STUDYING ABROAD
For Black Women

Diary of a Traveling Black Woman: A Guide to International Travel

Mini Travel Guide Series:

Dubai, Abu Dhabi & The 5 Other Emirates You Didn't Know About...

Jamaica: Likkle, but Tallawah!

Trinidad: More Than Just Carnival...

Iceland: Nature, Nurture, & Adventure

Solo Travel: Try It At Least Once!

and more...

Diary of a Traveling Black Woman:
A Guide to International Travel

"Mini Travel Guide Series"
Volume IV - Study Abroad
2nd Edition

Studying Abroad for Black Women

Adriana Smith

The Traveling Black Women Network
Grace Royal International, LLC
Atlanta, GA

Copyright ©2022 by Adriana Smith (2nd Edition)

All rights reserved. No part of this book may be reproduced by a mechanical, photographic, or electronic process; nor may any parts of this book be stored in any retrieval system without the written permission of the publisher-this excludes brief quotations used in reviews.

The intent of the author is to offer general information on studying abroad as a Black Woman. The author assumes no responsibility for the actions of the reader.

Cover Model: Adriana Smith
Cover Design: Nadine C. Duncan
Interior Design: Nadine C. Duncan

ISBN: 978-0578351070 (First Edition)
ISBN: 979-8-218-00376-0 (Second Edition)
ISBN: 9798218004224 (eBook)

1st Edition, July 2019
2nd Edition, May 2022
Travel Guide Series, Volume IV
Printed in the United States of America

Published in the United States by:
The Traveling Black Women Network
Grace Royal International, LLC
Atlanta, GA 30316

www.travelingblackwomen.com

For every first generation college student just trying to figure it out.

Contents

Dear Black Woman...13

What is Study Abroad?...17

Why Study Abroad as a Black Woman...34

Secure the "Study Abroad" Bag...47

Preparation Season...65

What to Expect...93

Pros & Cons for Black Women...98

Resources for Your Identities...108

Get to Know Your Host City...115

Find the Good in Good Bye...120

Additional Resources...134

About the Author...146

Dear Black Woman,

Picture this:

You're alone in Madrid. Standing on a busy street, with small cars zooming past, and Spaniards whizzing by on their way to wherever. Most likely work because it's about 10:25 am Madrid time. You look left and right and can't find your study abroad group leader or peers. All you remember is that everyone was supposed to meet in the hotel lobby at 10:40 am. Or was it 10:20 am? Dang. You can't remember now because the information given by the orientation leaders was in Spanish. Darn language skills. *Shouldn't you be fluent now?* You ask yourself.

Maybe everyone is at the nearest site that's likely on your tour schedule today. What was it again? Were we going to the Art Museum or the Palace? Should I go left or right?

You run to the intersection and don't know which way to go. A few seconds later, you see an older gentlemen approaching. Not sure what to do next, you run to him and begin to speak Spanish. At least you hope you can. Unable to get the words out, you move on and panic. "Where are they?"

If this was you, what would you do next?

This scenario occurred on my very first study abroad experience in Spain. Actually two days into my program, I had gotten lost in the streets of Madrid. Frustrated and discouraged, I continued pursuing my group for the next twenty minutes. And guess what? I still didn't find them. At that very moment, I felt defeated. I had traveled over 3,000 miles to experience Spain and I had failed already. And now, I wanted to return home two days into my study abroad program.

Honestly, if I had the money, I would've hopped on another plane and jetted out of Madrid so fast. There wouldn't have been anything that could've stopped me from tucking my tail and heading home. Luckily, however, I couldn't afford another plane ticket. I had already spent $1,000 for my flight. So instead, I walked back to the hotel to wait for the next tour. But, just so you know, my day was about to get worse.

Study abroad, from what I had gathered on the second day, was much more than being in a classroom. I had my first lesson in humility and culture shock. I had proclaimed Madrid a carbon copy of Miami, the center of the world. Of course, everyone knew about Miami. Who wouldn't? But, I soon realized that the people in Spain did not care about Miami like I did. It wasn't THEIR home. The citizens cared about their own city, country, and people. I entered another place and arrogantly expected it to be like home. Essentially, I disrespected THEM and THEIR country.

If I had to re-label this experience, it wouldn't have been called sTuDy AbRoAd. But rather the, "Get out your comfort zone experience." Or maybe the, "You might run or cry, but did you die? experience."

"Study Abroad is the opportunity to earn academic credit while taking courses at an institution outside of your home country."

So...
What is Study Abroad, Really?

Most colleges and universities host a list of study abroad programs that take place in various countries around the world. Through these programs, institutions have arranged for students to take a number of courses in exchange for credits toward their degree. There are various types of study abroad programs, but what you choose is determined by your interests.

So, study abroad is this —
THE WORLD AS YOUR CLASSROOM.

Typically, you learn about concepts, theories, languages, ideas, and historical facts and figures from your professor, textbook, and a range of sources. Yet, what you learn in a classroom is a fraction of what it takes to be "a knowledgeable and an effective citizen." Think about the people you will interact or do business with, or the unfamiliar places and cultures you will see. That's a skill in itself.

Going abroad hands you life lessons on top of academic and professional growth. It's through these international experiences that you can immerse yourself in a new culture. Your ability to navigate these experiences is a fundamental part of college and life.

So, study abroad is NOT:
- An extended vacation
- Opportunity to escape your academics
- Free time
- A sabbatical

And, study abroad is NOT designed to:
- Delay graduation
- Cost an arm and a leg
- Exclude students based on resources, background, or identity

It's more than that...

Study abroad, especially for Black Women, is this...

> Fortunately, I believe that my experiences being a minority has only strengthened my study abroad experience and given me a richer perspective on the world...While studying abroad, I have learned and felt that my cul-

ture is interesting, unique and important to the world. It is an integral piece of American culture as a whole.

- Joy Donnelly, studied abroad in Italy

The lasting lessons I learned had nothing to do with supply chain management, but with really submerging yourself in someone else's culture. I have the memories of struggling through the marché and having my classmates rely on my broken French. I remember being bombarded with questions from people in Turkey about my hair and my skin. In this day and age, I believe it's important for young people to experience the world for themselves... My only regret is that I didn't do more than one trip.

- Tiara Courtney, studied abroad in France & Turkey

In African countries, I felt like I was going to a family reunion. Folks thought I spoke the language, and that I looked like a cousin and it felt great. The diaspora is extraordinary.

- Nelda Dafinis, studied abroad in S. Africa & Namibia

Studying abroad was an eye-opening experience and quite shocking. As a first-generation college student and a minority, sometimes we know little to nothing about what studying abroad means. [But] with so many perks that came along with studying abroad such as building a great network of life long friends, new opportunities to travel around my host country and also majority of the region (Southeast Asia), learning new skills but ultimately personal growth.

- Brenda Namwawu, studied abroad in Hong Kong

"If everything was perfect, you would never learn and you would never grow."
- Beyoncé

Are you ready to make that decision? What will that look like for you? 5,4,3,2,1…Let's Go!

My Split-Second Decision to Study Abroad

The concept of study abroad was new to me. I hadn't a clue that it even existed. As a first-generation college student, at that time, I was more focused on doing well. Many first-time, underrepresented college students are not aware of the resources or opportunities afforded to them to study abroad. My opportunity came through a classroom visit from a study abroad advisor.

On this particular and ordinary day, I was working with my classmates on an assignment in my Spanish class. Ten minutes into the assignment, a tall, slim, white lady with short blonde hair walked into the class. As a sidenote, you'll find that the majority of study abroad students turn professionals are white and female.

My professor introduced her in English and revealed that she was a study abroad advisor. Those words "study abroad" didn't mean anything to me until this advisor began talking.

She began rambling off a list of study abroad programs and summer opportunities. What caught my ear was the mention of a 6-week summer program in Spain. Prior to this day, I had never even considered going abroad. The farthest I had ever been from home was college--a six-hour drive from Miami to Gainesville, FL. Now, I was thinking about leaving the country? This was unbelievable.

Yet, I had already contemplated adding Spanish as my second major about a month before. And, I needed a sequence of courses to make it happen. This summer program had begun to sound like Christmas. And, the stars were aligning, I thought.

While she continued to provide details about the program, it took me a split second to decide to apply and participate in this new idea called study abroad. I hadn't even considered one major challenge and complication: *my mom.*

To be continued…

***

Are you ready to Level Up?

Deciding to study abroad can be an exciting, yet scary moment of your life. You're asking yourself to take a risk and totally go somewhere new for a period of time. Whether you've traveled abroad or not, studying abroad is a different beast. It's more to going abroad than purchasing a ticket and hopping on the plane. It demands initiative and discipline in order to complete the required applications and documentation.

Most importantly, you will have to study. It's not a sponsored vacation, but rather, an opportunity to see the world through your studies.

Choose Your Study Abroad Life

In a moment, I want you to close your eyes and think about the city or country you've always wanted to see and explore. The location that has been on your bucket list since you were young. And, the country that you would travel to if cost wasn't a factor.

Ok, now, close your eyes and picture that place. (I'm serious.)

Where is it? What country or city did you picture?

Write it here:

_____

> *Cue Ariana Grande*
> "I see it. I like it. I want it. I got it."

Now, that place you've just listed is where you should start. Study abroad is about making dreams come true. It's about fulfilling lifelong goals alongside your pursuit of your college degree. They say college is the best years of your life. But, I say that college is the BEGINNING of the best years of life. Why? Because college grooms you and nurtures the person you are to become. Why else have an office or contact that solely advises students on studying abroad? The faculty and staff at your college are dedicated to your success. You just have to take advantage.

So now that you've chosen a location, you now have to select a program that will fit your desires, course requirements, and budget. You won't need to know all of these answers because your study abroad office is setup to provide individual assessments and advising sessions to get you started.

Please be mindful that some colleges

may not have study abroad programs in your desired destination. But, if your study abroad office is anything like mine, then there may be a few options in YOUR dream country.

Here are your options:

If you're super adventurous and independent, you might opt to study abroad for a semester or year. There are a few ways to do so. One might be that you participate in an exchange program where you switch places with a student at a foreign institution. It's not literally switching lives (or bodies like in Freaky Friday with Lindsay Lohan), but for a duration of time, you and another student spend time at each other's universities.

You're expected to be more independent and proactive. You won't have someone everyday to guide your decisions or actions. You are really a student in your host university and treated like a native student there.

If you're a bit shy or intimidated by an exchange program, and there's nothing wrong with that, then you probably should choose a customizable program administered by an outside company. Unlike exchange programs that are operated by your on-campus study abroad office, these providers are typically private organizations that create specific programs for your college.

Some students prefer to participate with private companies like ISA, IES Abroad, and CIEE. These companies provide 24/7 care and support wherever they host their programs. They may also have more program selections than your university. So, although your study abroad advisor would love to travel abroad with you and be of assistance when you need them, they unfortunately cannot. They have to tend to dozens, maybe even hundreds of students like you. These companies, however, usually have on-site campuses, housing, and offices just for you. If you ever have an issue, you can contact them very easily in-country, rather than wait several hours or days later for the office back home to respond to you.

What if you don't want to study abroad for a whole semester or year?

If it's too long or you have obligations that get in the way of you studying abroad that long, then you can travel with your faculty and peers. This short-term, faculty-led program option can range from one week, two weeks, or up to several weeks. The duration depends on the faculty and the program that they've created. Students love this option because they (1) find security being with people they know; (2) receive course credit for a short period of time; (3) play a sport and can't commit to longer programs, and/or (4) can avoid FOMO (fear of missing out). Some of these short-term programs may occur during the winter term, spring break, at the end of May (known as Maymesters) and summer.

You have the power to decide which time of year is best for you. Don't feel overwhelmed or discouraged if you feel that there are too many options. In fact, after reviewing the types of programs above, ask yourself the following questions. This way you can identify which programs you're interested in and begin to list what it'll take to apply and participate.

I ask my students to begin thinking about planning for their study abroad experience at least a year in advance. There's so much to consider, but before we get to all of that, here are some questions to ask yourself:

- What are your goals?
- Where do you want to go and when?

- Are you eligible?
- Do you meet the minimum GPA requirements?
- Do you meet the language requirements (if applicable)?
- What year are you?
- Will you be affected academically being away for a semester or year?
- How much will the program cost?
- How will you fund this program?
  - Scholarships?/Grants?
  - Part-time/Full-time Job?
  - Family?
- What are you most afraid of?
- What are some of your concerns about studying abroad?
- How can you address them?
  - Your health
  - Your safety
  - What could stop you from doing the work necessary to study abroad?

Notice any underlying themes or connections? If you notice that you won't have much funding or support, you might choose a cheaper or shorter study abroad program. If you lack the language skills, you can select programs taught in English. Find out what works for YOU.

But, what if your institution doesn't have a study abroad office?

Here's what you can do:

1. Express your interest and desire to study abroad to your academic and/or faculty advisor. Ask for assistance and determine whether they are willing to help you through the process.
2. Use study abroad search engines and platforms: GoAbroad and IIE Program Directory to browse destinations and programs.
3. Filter through programs that will meet your standards and academic requirements.
4. Share this list of programs with advisor and see which is the best fit.
5. Meet with a Financial Aid Counselor about prospective programs and whether you're eligible to receive aid.
6. Talk to your peers about their study abroad experience and in which programs they participated.
7. Once program and location are selected, begin to communicate with program

provider AND apply.
8. Submit necessary documents and obtain acceptance packet.
9. Confirm and finalize your plans with your advisor. There may be documents you need to submit to your institution.
10. Follow the steps in the welcome packet, including obtaining a passport and/or visa.
11. Prepare to study abroad!

Sis, you got this!

Studying abroad in Santander, Spain
Circa 2009

Why Study Abroad as a Black Woman?

It's simple. Of the 300,000 students who studied abroad in 2018, 6% of those who participated identified as Black/African-American, a very low number compared to the 71% who identified as White. 67% of the US students who studied abroad were women. So study abroad is very white and female.

To be honest, there aren't any statistics that share how many BLACK women study abroad. While the future is female, we still can't be surprised at the lack of representation within these educational communities and opportunities.

In my own experiences studying abroad, I was the only Black student in my program. This was out of a group of twenty. Twenty?! I felt isolated, alone, hidden and a bit overlooked. Everyone else benefited from a privilege of having traveled abroad with their family before, so they couldn't understand or relate to little ol' me when I was having a mini panic attack for being far away from home.

Oh, and don't think that going off to

graduate school is any different. When I studied abroad in Madrid through New York University for my one-year master's program, I had been one of three black students on the program. Luckily, I met another Black woman, Tiffany, who I love and adore.

This shows you just how precious it is being a Black Woman abroad. How likely is it that you will meet another Black woman in your program? To tell you the truth, it's minimal. And, to top it off, the citizens in these different countries are either mesmerized or disgusted by our presence. But, that doesn't matter. In a world where our melanin, hair, and Black beauty are mocked, mimicked, and ridiculed, remember this:

"You should never view your challenges as a disadvantage. Instead, it's important for you to understand that your experience facing and overcoming adversity is actually one of your biggest advantages."
- Michelle Obama

Studying abroad as a Black Woman develops your confidence in so many ways. Not to say that your confidence is not already on level Beyonce, but you walk a little differently when you've traveled internationally.

Today, I attribute my language skills, employability, and global citizenry to this exact opportunity. Studying abroad in college has defined my professional career and who I am as a Black Woman. More importantly, as the only Black student in my program, I had a chance to represent for people like me. And, to appreciate what so many students and people of color don't get to do.

Although I had moments of loneliness, homesickness and culture shock, I could never regret my study abroad experience. And as a first-generation college graduate and study abroad alum, I now get to promote study abroad to students. I remind them, especially students of color, that the time is NOW.

Studying abroad enhances your skill set and it creates a dialogue about differences, appreciation for cultures and people, and expands our territory. I could only imagine what my life would be like if I hadn't studied abroad…
Nah, nevermind. I can't.

And besides, how can you "run the world," when you've never seen it?

*"I'm repping for the girls
Who taking over the world
Have me raise a glass
For the college grads"*

-Beyonce, "Run the world"

"Please, don't go!" -Your parents

Remember that complication that I had to deal with once I decided I wanted to study abroad? Yes? Well, you may be hesitant to ask your parent(s). Whether you're a product of a single parent home or not, I'm here to tell you that it's not as bad as you may think.

Here's what happened to me once I decided to study abroad:

When the advisor ended her speech, I convinced myself that I wanted to not only take the two summer courses, but also gain Spanish fluency and see the world. In hindsight, I didn't know I would gain so much more from this opportunity.

Immediately after class ended, I rushed to my dorm room, opened my laptop, went to the website, and applied. "What just happened?" - I asked myself. I really didn't think it through, but I knew that it was the right move.

This all took about an hour and 15 minutes. The time to finish class, walk to my room, and apply changed my life forever. A day later, I met with the study abroad advisor to confirm my participation. I also met with a financial aid advisor to ensure my scholarship would fund the program.

The biggest challenge was yet to come. Later that day, I called my mom to inform her of my decision to study abroad in Spain. And well...

Even though I didn't know what to say, my heart wouldn't let her deter me. When she picked up, I nervously begin the conversation by saying, "Hey mom, guess where I'm going this summer?" My mom is not one for games so she quickly and annoyingly said, "Where?!"

"SPAIN!" - I blurted.

If you were there, you would've heard the crickets on the other side of the phone. There was complete silence. Believe it or not, my single-mother of seven children was apprehensive about me going. Still to this day, she has never flown on a plane or traveled outside of the US. Of course she would be afraid! But I knew I couldn't let her fears stop me. There was this fire and desire in me to see what the rest of the world was like. Remember: I didn't ask. I just told her.

Maybe your parent(s), or family, will eventually get on board like mine. Or, maybe not. That's ok! Your parents' support shouldn't dictate your decision to study abroad.

Sidenote: I also don't want you to get in trouble as I know how sensitive it is to tell your mom what YOU plan to do.
#dontgetyourfeelingshurt

I literally had my mom ask me not to study abroad in Spain. This was hurtful. Although this was my second time going abroad, she couldn't help but be fearful about what was portrayed in the media. But, after my return, and years of professional experience, she has finally recognized the reward. When I asked my mom about her thoughts now that she knows about study abroad, she said:

"I had to trust that she knew what she wanted and needed for her path and life. She was getting experience and fulfilling a lifelong dream of traveling. I was amazed at the woman she was becoming because of this experience that, at first, seemed very scary and dangerous.

Now, I know that it was the right move for my daughter."

So, how do you get your parent(s) or guardian(s) comfortable with the idea of studying abroad??? According to Former First Lady, Michelle Obama:

"One of the things that we really need to do is to provide more information for parents so they have an understanding why study abroad is important, how it's going to expand the opportunities for their loved ones and how are they going to be able to afford it."

Tip #1:
- Give them information. Pamphlets, flyers, website links, or the contact information of your study abroad advisor.

Tip #2:
- Look up potential scholarships or grants for study abroad. THERE'S MONEY TO BE USED JUST FOR YOU. Show them that you've found a plan to cover a por-

tion or all of costs of the program. We understand our parents' finances more than anyone. Let them know that we are considerate and able to find ways to pay for it ourselves.

Tip #3:

- Share with them how study abroad correlates with your goals. Don't be shy about what and who you want to become. As Mrs. Obama says "I want more young people like you to take that step. Try something new, travel abroad."

Tip #4:

- Answer the following questions using your study abroad advisor/representative, financial aid counselors, and online resources. Then, show the checklist to your parent(s) while discussing your desire to study abroad.

  1. Do I know someone else who has studied abroad? Yes No
  2. If yes, then who? _____
  3. How long will I be abroad?

4. Will I be going with a faculty? Yes No
   5. If no, then who? (Professor, program, or contact) _____
   6. Will I be covered with health/medical insurance?_____
   7. If yes, how much will it cost? _____
   8. What does it cover? _____

Mrs. Obama continues:

> "They also need to understand more about an ever-globalizing economy and that traveling abroad is no longer just a nice thing to do; it's becoming more and more a central part of a student's educational experience."

THIS.

Besides, you don't want to disappoint the FIRST Black First Lady of the United States, do you?!

Your Checklist:

- [ ] Meet with a study abroad advisor.
- [ ] Choose a destination and program.
- [ ] Get approval from your academic advisor.
- [ ] Complete your application by deadline.
- [ ] GET ACCEPTED TO STUDY ABROAD!
- [ ] Secure the necessary documentation.
- [ ] Confirm your travel plans.

Then comes the important part...

Day trip to Toledo, Spain.

Secure the "Study Abroad" Bag

Whether you like it or not, everything costs money. And, whether you have it or not, when you have an expense, you will have to pay it.

Thankfully, you're reading this guide, which means you are already thinking about securing your plans and bag. I, personally, didn't have this type of guidance. If I did, I wouldn't have been in Spain (the second time) broke and begging for money to pay rent. Don't do as I did, do as I would do NOW!!

Costs to Consider

The various types of study abroad programs are considerably different in program cost. Usually the most affordable option would be the exchange programs since they're hosted by your home university. Costs are comparable to what you pay for a regular semester, whereas programs that involved faculty or customized programs will definitely cost more.

Be mindful also about whether you can

cover your program with financial aid. If you receive scholarships, grants, and funding from private sources, you might be able to use them for these internal programs. Additional costs would be your passport, visa (if applicable), plane ticket, and maybe spending money while abroad.

This isn't always the case when you decide to study abroad. If you participate in customized or faculty-led programs, your financial aid may or may not apply to its coverage. If it falls outside of the two semesters, Fall and Spring, then you're responsible to cover any short-term study abroad programs during the winter, spring, Maymester and summer terms.

You must maintain full-time status while abroad. Failure to do so could jeopardize your financial eligibility and enrollment in your study abroad program. Check your school's policy!

Students tend to take out student loans to cover the cost of these programs, which could range from $4,000 (short-term) to over $20,000 (customized semester). These would be out-of-pocket expenses in addition to the fees that you'll need to cover at your home institution.

I wouldn't recommend taking out a loan

(or maybe another) to pay for your experience. Rather, I would highly suggest you speak to a financial aid counselor and study abroad advisor for more appropriate options for you. They will have resources and information regarding institutional and national scholarships that you might qualify for. As a Black Woman, there are dozens of scholarships waiting to pay for your study abroad experience.

I've been told that as a woman of color, I shouldn't have to spend a dime for higher education. Keep this in mind before taking out a loan that will be around for a long time.

Now, consider the following program fees and expenses. Here you'll get a general idea of which program is right for you.

Breathe, it will be ok!

The following templates don't include additional fees, such as books and supplies, fees for special courses, personal and travel expenses, or emergency funds. Still include these costs. Doing so will alleviate any stress in the first few and crucial weeks of your time abroad.

Plan ahead now so you can enjoy later!

Exchange program being considered (Name program or country):

_____

Expense	*Cost*
Application fee/Deposit:	
Full program fee	
Housing & Meals fee *(if not included in program fee)*	
Airfare/Transportation	
Passport and visa fees	
Immunizations	
Health coverage *(if not included in program fee)*	
Total	

Additional Costs to Consider:

Exchange program being considered (Name program or country):

_____

Expense	Cost
Application fee/Deposit:	
Full program fee	
Housing & Meals fee *(if not included in program fee)*	
Airfare/Transportation	
Passport and visa fees	
Immunizations	
Health coverage *(if not included in program fee)*	
Total	

Additional Costs to Consider:

Customized program being considered:

_____

Expense	*Cost*
Application fee/Deposit:	
Full program fee	
Housing & Meals fee *(if not included in program fee)*	
Airfare/Transportation	
Passport and visa fees	
Immunizations	
Health coverage *(if not included in program fee)*	
Total	

Additional Costs to Consider:

Faculty-led Program being considered:

_____

Expense	Cost
Application fee/Deposit:	
Full program fee	
Housing & Meals fee *(if not included in program fee)*	
Airfare/Transportation	
Passport and visa fees	
Immunizations	
Health coverage *(if not included in program fee)*	
Total	

Additional Costs to Consider:

Other Program being considered:

_____

Expense	*Cost*
Application fee/Deposit:	
Full program fee	
Housing & Meals fee *(if not included in program fee)*	
Airfare/Transportation	
Passport and visa fees	
Immunizations	
Health coverage *(if not included in program fee)*	
Total	

Additional Costs to Consider:

Financial Planning Tips:

Take baby steps when planning to study abroad. Remember, you're also taking classes and doing a million of other tasks during the semester.

Start with these five steps:

1. *Research:* Seek out an advisor or someone who has knowledge of your study abroad program and the day-to-day costs in the country. Don't only rely on someone else's word or account of a country. A quick google search will bring you pages of information about what you want to know.

2. *Plan for what you know:* Start with the costs that you know you will have to plan for. These will be expected costs like the program fee, airfare, housing, tuition, etc.

3. *Plan for what you need (and want):* List the additional things

you will need money for like fare for transportation around the city, books and supplies, laundry, and international cell phone service. Also include traveling during breaks and holidays, souvenirs, eating out, entertainment—activities that will make your time abroad much more enjoyable.

4. The Essentials: Before you leave for your program, make a list of the items that you probably won't be able to get abroad. Hair and beauty products for Black Women are sometimes hard to find once in your host city.

5. Emergency Funds: This was saved for last, not because it wasn't important, but because this might be the hardest to budget for as a college student... especially, if you do not have the financial support from family due to personal circumstances OR, limited scholarship and financial aid. Whatever the case may be, I urge you to include this in your study abroad budget. Save an amount that is substantial, but also flexible in case something goes wrong.

Examples of emergencies include a medical bill, lost luggage, emergency accommodation, lost passport, or anything else.

Do you really need an emergency fund?

I kind of wished I'd started an emergency fund when I studied abroad the second time. I was broke the first month of the program and felt guilty for turning new friends down for a night out. More importantly, I was super stressed out financially because I needed to pay rent for my homestay.

So yes! There is no way to make this any clearer. Most of us don't get serious about saving until later in life. I'm not advising you to save a million dollars, but I'm urging you to grow a small fund to avoid any headaches on your study abroad program. I'm trying to help you avoid any added stress while abroad. You'll be stressed enough just being away from your friends, family, significant other, cat, dog, etc. for an extended period of time.

If you need some quick tips, don't skip this section.
- Start small.

- Overestimate what you think you'll need.
- Open a Separate Account for Your Fund
- Fund the Account Regularly
- Remember the Fund is meant to be Flexible

What's your goal?

$ _____

Funded by when: _____

What steps will you take to get there? (Write them in the space below.)

Join Black travel communities, like Traveling Black Women, for the latest tips on your potential study abroad destination.

Bad N' Budgeting

1. ***Low Cost Flights:*** Decide the best method of transportation to your host city. If you're living in the Northern US and studying abroad in Canada, you may opt to take a train or drive across the border to your destination. Of course, if you're studying abroad on a different continent, then you have to hop on a plane. You might think you will have to shell out $2,000 for a flight, but that's not true. As a college student, you have the pleasure of getting special discounts from travel companies like StudentUniverse and STA Travel. Sign up to their newsletter and track the amazing flight deals across the world.

2. ***Passport/Visa:*** If you don't already have a passport, then apply now. There's no need to wait until the last minute to get one. The cost will significantly rise the closer you get to your program start date. In order to apply for your visa, you need your passport. No passport, no visa. Get it started now. Simply, talk to your study abroad advisor, or visit the US Depart-

ment of State website for more information.

3. *Cook for yourself:* While away from the food you're used to, or comfort foods that make you smile, there's a chance you have to provide your own meals. This tip excludes programs that include meals. If your study abroad program doesn't have a meal option, then you're left to decide how you're going to feed yourself. The easiest option is to eat out every day, but that's not affordable since most local restaurants may charge you at least $10+/meal. The more economic decision is to grocery shop and cook your own meals. Save that money for a weekend trip to another country. Eeooww!

4. *Your Hair:* If there's a specific brand that you can't live without, then plan to take all that you need for the time that you're away. You might think that ordering it online and having it mailed to you abroad will save you. It won't! When you factor in the cost of shipping internationally and the weight of the package, plus possible Customs fees, you might as well book a flight. See the packing guide for

tips of what to bring with you vs what you can buy abroad.

Tip #1:

Travel abroad with a protective style. Braids, Crochet, or sew-in.

Tip #2:

If you're a risk taker and would rather wait until you're in your host city, then find the nearest African community. There is where you'll discover your beloved hair products, beauty salons, and stylists to do your hair.

A major part of your journey abroad is maintaining your sanity; including keeping your budget and finances in check.

Can't Get Enough? More Financial Planning Tips

Can I use my debit or credit card abroad? Yes and No. Well, it depends.

We live in a digital world. Cash is useful, but it's definitely not as valuable as the plastic cards in your wallet right now. But that doesn't mean that sort of thinking will apply while you're abroad. Most places prefer cash and don't have access to swipe your debit or credit card. You'll need to be flexible about how you spend and make purchases abroad.

Prior to departing, speak to a financial advisor at your bank and/or a representative at your credit card company. A conversation with a financial planner will put you at ease once they explain your options for spending and purchasing internationally. For example, swiping your card in another country doesn't provide the same pleasure while here in the US. Let's say you need to make a withdrawal from an international ATM, you may be charged a fee for the money you're withdrawing. Check out the banks listed in the followed table and see the foreign transaction and withdrawal fees. Fees by the non-US Bank operator may also apply.

Bank Institution	Debit Card Foreign Transaction Fees	Foreign ATM Withdrawal Cost
Bank of America	3%	$5+3% of amount
Chase Bank	3%	$5+3% of amount
CitiBank	3%	$2.50+3% of amount
TD Bank	None	3%
Wells Fargo	3%	$5+3% of amount

*Information gathered from NerdWallet

Contacting your bank before leaving will ensure you have access to your money at all times. If you don't inform them of your travel plans, they may freeze your accounts because of foreign transactions or what they think may be fraudulent activity. It's better for you to just communicate with them to avoid any mishap abroad.

Oh, and you may want to have one or two back up cards because you wouldn't want your main card to get chewed up by the ATM. #Truestory

Preparation Season

Previously published on www.Travepreneur.com
"Can't Figure Out Where To Begin Your Travel Plans? Start Here."
Edited, modified and formatted for the purpose of this book.

Don't want to search millions of posts just to plan your trip? Let's start with the basics: Health, Safety, Travel Planning, Travel Apps, Blogs and Communities.

This will get you started in the right direction of your travel planning process and establish a foundation.

How to use:
- Start from the beginning and take it one step at a time.
- Skip around as needed.
- Go directly to a section.
- Refer a friend.
- Use this guide as a checklist.

Shall we begin?

Travel Health

Health abroad is just as important as health coverage in your own country. Not only do you need to protect yourself medically, but you'll also need to prepare in case of an emergency.

This isn't to jinx you, but it is likely that something IS going to happen. In case of sickness or death (yes, death), you are prepared and won't have to pay out-of-pocket for expenses you didn't plan for. (Like paying $40,000 to have your body or a family member's body sent back home.)

Thankfully, your study abroad program will include health coverage that will allow you to seek medical attention while abroad. If you're suffering through an illness, please disclose any physical, personal, and mental health information. This will help your advisors plan and maintain a safe and health program experience for you.

Travel Vaccinations

Even before boarding your plane, you need to ask yourself: What vaccines or medicines will I need for my trip?

These resources specify, by country, what is required, recommended, and encouraged for you to take. Pay attention to the CDC's travel health information. And, visit the Passport Health clinic for your vaccinations and GoodRx for prescription drugs.

Centers for Disease Control and Prevention: Use the CDC travel health resource to learn which travel vaccines or medicines you'll need for your trip abroad. Since the pandemic in 2020, regulations can change rapidly. Always check for the most up-to-date policies on the government websites for your destination.

Passport Health: Schedule an appointment at a local travel health clinic to get your required vaccinations before arrival in your destination.

GoodRx: Looking for the best prices on prescription drugs? With the access of over 75,000 pharmacies, you can find coupons and discounts on medicines needed for your trips abroad.

Travel Insurance

"Is travel insurance worth it?" – I would ask myself before purchasing a flight.

"Nah," I would respond.

But, seeing multiple accounts of people opting out of travel insurance and spending thousands on flight cancellations, ticket changes, medical bills, and sending the body of a loved one home, that has been my cue to be responsible. Or rather, be better prepared.

As a study abroad student, I don't want an emergency to come about without any support or advanced preparation. Invest in travel insurance. Purchase a plan per trip, annually, or whatever is suitable for you. Some credit card companies offer travel insurance. Talk to a bank representative to ensure that they have the appropriate travel coverage. If you don't, compare plans online.

Here are a few examples that you can look into:

World Nomads: Get insurance coverage while exploring the world. You don't want to get caught up or risk being abroad in an emergency without some sort of protection.

Travel Medical Insurance: Search insurance options and purchase a plan that's right for you when you travel. Don't leave without protection.

InsureMyTrip: If you have a cancellation or interruption on your trip, you'd want to be protected and covered by insurance. Get a quote to compare your insurance needs and budget.

Stressed AF?: Mental Health Tips for Black Women

> "Only make decisions that support your self-image, self-esteem, and self-worth." - Oprah Winfrey

You can't escape your emotional or mental health issues by studying abroad. Life continues to happen, and adding a new stressor, like going abroad, can worsen your symptoms and health.

This isn't meant to diagnose you or make you feel like you're not worthy of a study abroad experience. Instead, this is to encourage you to look inward and make sure you're healthy to live and study in a new environment. Seeking mental and medical attention is a courageous decision, especially as a Black Woman who is often told "to pray," "snap out of it," or that "therapists are for white people."

Don't prolong seeking treatment on the account of family pressure or stigma. Do you, boo!

Now, while emotional and mental health problems will look differently for everyone. Here are some tips to remain mentally, emotionally, and physically sound while studying abroad.

1. Don't play hide and seek with your emotions. Instead, be open and honest with yourself and your study abroad advisor and leaders.
2. Breathe Deep. You know that phrase, "Think before you speak?" Well, breathe before you panic. Give yourself 5 to 10 seconds of deep breaths that will help reduce your anxiety and heart rate.
3. Get Social (For the extroverts). Join a local organization, sport, or club and connect with new people and ideas.
4. Explore a new hobby (For the introverts). This doesn't involve social interaction or spending time in a social setting. You can pick and choose how you learn your new skill.
5. Stay connected to positive influences. This may be tricky because sometimes our friends and family aren't always the most positive or supportive. Studying abroad is already stressful. When you need to

most, limit your interactions with negative people and situations. Surround yourself with those who will be your champions.

Here are some additional resources:

- *Education Abroad* - Mental Health and Study Abroad: Responding to the Concern
- *GoOverseas* - How to Deal With Depression While Studying Abroad
- *University of Michigan* - Resilient Traveling Safety

Health and safety are like fraternal twins. Two distinct topics that stem from the same concept of emergency preparedness. There is not one without the other, so I included them together before we get into travel planning and resources.

Most times, we like to start the travel planning process before we gather background information about the destination itself. Usually, we delve into health and safety once we've secured our flights, booked our accommodations, and have applied for our visas.

But, I believe travel safety shouldn't be overlooked or left to the last minute to consider. Health AND safety should be the first to review.

Advisory & Alerts

The US State Department travel advisory can determine whether we need to choose a completely different destination based on its recommendations, evaluations, and warnings. Reviewing security and medical alerts in a destination may also allow us to better understand the local conditions before we get there. No money is lost or no trying to convince ourselves to go.

I encourage you to use the following safety sites, communities, and alerts to plan ahead for your future trips. These take into consideration terrorism, political climate, health and disease risks, severe weather, living conditions, and security in each country around the world.

The programs that have been developed and advertised at your institution have been vetted and evaluated for maximized safety and support. The extra precaution will help you determine your comfort zone, as well as your parents.

- *STEP: Smart Traveler Enrollment Program:* Register your trips online. Receive safety and emergency updates about your destination from the US Embassy.

- *US State Department Travel Advisory:* If you want to know how safe a country is at the time, use the travel advisory for guidance. The description for each country details how to take precaution while traveling.

- *Depart Smart:* Are you prepared when you travel abroad? Take the Travel Safety Training to ensure you are.

- *Your Local Fire Department:* (Free Response Training/CERT Training) Interested in putting together an emergency or survival kit? Or, learn more about emergency preparedness? Seek professional help from your local fire department. They usually have free emergency response training during the week.

- *Travel Risk Map:* At a glance, you can

view the security risks, ranging from insignificant to extreme in the world. Like the Travel Advisory, you'll be guided on how to assess whether you should avoid specific countries. Included are medical and road safety assessments in each country.

- *Safe Travel USA:* Road tripping around the US? Stay updated with road hazards, traffic, weather, and conditions that can affect your travel plans. Don't hit the road without your handy, dandy road safety site.

- *MaidenVoyage:* While it's a network for professional businesswomen, the site features a list of certified female-friendly hotels and city guides.

- *Jozu For Women:* A community of women dedicated to creating & maintaining a safe travel space for others. They provide safety tips, travel advice and network.

- *Wandersafe:* This safety tool and app advises you in real-time about what's happening in your area. Periodically, there will be check-ins to ask: "Do you feel safe?"

- *Pathways to Safety International:* If you are involved in interpersonal or gender-based violence abroad, Pathways offer 24/7 support and assistance regardless of where you are in the world.

Travel Planning

Planning made easy? Or at least simplified. You won't have to leave this page to plan your upcoming trip. Promise. I've listed various sites that'll allow you to plan for weather/seasons and your budget, purchase cheap flights, read reviews on hotels or restaurants, and get expert advice for your destination.

Listen, at least you don't have to spend hours on Google getting to these resources.

- *Around the World:* Need to know when to go where? Don't worry. Always know the best time of year to travel the world.

- *Seasons Around the World:* If you're conscious of the weather, then peek at the recommendations on where to go and when.

- *TripAdvisor:* Why not rely on others' opinions about a restaurant, hotel, tour company, etc? It's useful. Especially now you can filter the reviews by traveler type (i.e. solo).

- *Scott's Cheap Flights:* (My fave!!) Get the cheapest flights to anywhere. Sign up for daily blasts and you just might catch a great deal. Hurry though. Those deals only last a few days.

- *Google Flights:* I only search for flights using this tool. It's simple, quick, and sometimes gives me the best rate compared to purchasing through a third-party company.

- *Google Trips:* Manage your trip itinerary in one place. Plan a specific one for yourself or use the recommendations as you travel about. Isn't Google the best?

- *TripSavvy:* Experts share their perspective as a local on what's happening in your destination. Unlike reviews from tourists, you get the in-country feedback and guidance on what to do, where to go, and how to spend your time while there.

- *Budget Your Trip:* All you have to do is search for your destination and get an instant budget guide on what you can expect to spend. Because budget is relative, you decide on your travel style (i.e. mid-range).

- *Timbuktu Travel:* Sometimes you don't want to do any planning. Just pick your destination and let someone else plan the trip for you. Search here to see which African countries you can go to through this company.

Social Impact Tourism Volunteer Abroad

Want to get more involved during your time abroad? If you are studying to be a graphic designer, an educator, or environmentalist, then you have the skills that many global organizations are seeking.

Browse the best volunteer abroad programs below to see how you can assist local organizations. Don't have the time to travel to the country? Volunteer online.

Recommendations:

- *GivingWay:* Want to dedicate your resources and skills to communities abroad? The platform connects prospective volunteers and organizations for free.

- *GoAbroad:* Looking for meaningful travel experiences around the world? Find opportunities to work abroad, volunteer abroad, intern abroad, or study abroad.

- *Hands-On Institute:* Work with various communities in Nepal. Passionate about women empowerment, civil rights, equality, education, sustainability? Plan your visit here.

Passport or Visa

We all ask this question: "Will I need a visa to travel to (insert country)?" With sites like Travisa, you can simply answer that question in a matter of seconds. US passport holders can travel to 177 countries without filling out any visa paperwork before arrival.

Yet, there are constantly updates regulated by each country and new requirements to be fulfilled. So, it doesn't hurt to review the websites below for updated information. In case a change has been made during the travel planning stages, you can adjust appropriately.

For most countries, you're not allowed to apply for the visa until you're within a certain amount of time of your trip. Plan accordingly and don't wait until the last minute to apply. Luckily, you can apply for a visa on arrival in some countries like Nepal. And, e-visas for places like India and Turkey.

- To apply for a new or renew your US passport, visit the US Department of State website.

- Travisa is a visa service for locations around the world. Need assistance either look to your study abroad advisor or Travisa!

- Want to speed through US customs when you've returned from abroad? Download this mobile app before you depart. Mobile Passport - Mobile Passport expedites your way through US customs. But only at select airports and cruise ports.

Accessories

Add accessories to your study abroad preparation list. These items are my favorite because I enjoy being organized, prepared, and at peace when I'm traveling. I'm sure you do too. As a student studying abroad, you have to look out for yourself, which is why having anti-theft items like a purse or money belt are so worth it.

Also, will you need a travel adapter or converter? Don't know. POWER PLUGS and SOCKETS OF THE WORLD is a database with each type of power socket for every destination. While you're shopping for these items (or creating your wishlist), don't forget to add one to your cart.

Packing:

- *Packing cubes:* You ever pack something and simply lose it in your luggage or it just wouldn't fit? Packing cubes are great additions to organize your stuff in your luggage. I never go without using my packing cubes because with only using a carry-on, I use every inch effectively.

- *Roll, roll, roll:* Roll your pants, roll your sweaters, roll your dresses, roll them all! Your clothing won't be as wrinkled than if you fold them. Roll them tightly and layer them as the bottom row. You can cram rolls of pants and bigger items in the crevices of your luggage much better.

- *Color coordinate:* Bring clothing and shoes that match with each other. Instead of bringing three pairs of shoes to match each of your outfits, bring one that matches them all. Just release your inner stylist. It'll work.

- *Consolidate your bags:* You're happier and stress-free with less bags. Having too many items and bags in your hands or possessions can result in losing them while traveling. Plus, you'd have to combine your luggage and bags when you board the plane anyway. One personal item and a carry-on. Might as well make that decision while you're packing.

- *Valuables:* Don't pack any valuables that you wouldn't want to get lost or stolen. If you don't want that to happen, don't take it with you.

Don't forget...

- Money Belt
- Power Sockets / Travel Adapters
- Anti-theft Purse

Money & Currency

Before anything else is done, please call your bank ASAP and inform them of your travel plans. If you bank with Wells Fargo, as I do, then you're able to submit your travel plans online.

Log into your account. Click on 'Travel Plans.' Enter your trip details, then hit submit. Your bank (Wells Fargo at least) now knows which cards will be used and where. No more blocked cards while traveling! Some banks have since updated this because of the frequency of travel. However, it doesn't hurt to check!

Currency Exchange

Now the second important question about money:

> "Should I convert money before or after I've arrived at my destination?"

While some may say have at least $200-$300 USD converted before you even touch down at the airport, others suggest converting currency at the airport or even withdrawing cash from an ATM upon arrival. Either way, decide which is the best option for you. Keep in mind, there will be different exchange rates and fees affiliated with each decision.

Using plastic would provide you with the best exchange rate without all the fees. Or, if you prefer to have the cash for those places that won't accept cards. To avoid any issues that can come up, check out the following money and currency resources:

- *Nerdwallet:* If you don't know which to choose: exchanging money before or after you arrive, read this for better insight.
- *Travelex:* Rather have the local currency before you jet off? Order the currency

online.

- *XE Currency:* There's no need to memorize the conversion rate in your local community with this app.

> *Always have a backup plan or source. You could be at risk of being stuck abroad without a source of money.*

Airport or Airline

Airports and airlines are as distinct as the countries that they're in. That is not a surprise but familiarity is comforting when sometimes you just want to know where the nearest lounge is or where to find a plug. Get all that and more with the following resources.

- *Seat Guru:* Window or the aisle seat? No more guessing at which seat is the best. Get reviews and updates about seats on different aircraft carriers and more.

- *Flio:* Don't ever miss a flight with status updates or miss a call because of a dead battery. Always know what's in and around the airport at all times.

- *Lounge Buddy:* Have access to lounges in airports across the world. Just search using the web or app, purchase a pass, and enjoy the lounge and its amenities.

Language Barrier

"How do I get past the language barrier?"

If you're considering traveling to a country where the people don't speak much English or you can't speak their language, here are a few resources and tips to help you feel more comfortable.

- *Duolingo:* Before you leave for your trip, download this free resource assisting language learners through fun and interactive exercises.

- *Google Translate:* You'll have access to the app whether you have WiFi or not. So if you need to translate a sign, just hold your phone up, touch the screen, and it will be translated.

- *Google Pixel Buds:* Even if you know the basics, you probably won't be able to have a full conversation with someone. With these headphones, however, you'll get a real-time translation.

Whether you download these apps or buy the headphones, you should always learn some basics. Not only to make a purchase, order food items, or ask where something is, but also because it shows your appreciation for the local language. Don't fall into the trap thinking everyone knows English or that they should. Getting around can be challenging especially in rural communities and countries without much access to the language.

Memorize, write down or save these common phrases or words in your host language:

Good Morning / Afternoon / Evening
Please / Thank you
How Much?
Toilet / Restroom
Yes / No
Help

Travel Planning Apps

Clear off space on your phone for some (maybe not all) of these apps. Depending on your trip and where you're going, you might need these apps at different times.

Safety App? Check!
What to do. What to see App? Check!
Afraid of flying App? Check!
There is an app for everything.

Recommended Travel Apps:
- BSafe
- Wandersafe
- Headspace
- Travefy
- TripIt
- Flio
- Lounge Buddy
- XE Currency
- Flush*

Not available in the US iTunes Store.

Stay Connected

The first and last time I used my phone

abroad, I racked up to $900 worth of roaming and data fees. Never again!

Cell phone providers have done much better since that time. They now offer specific international phone plans that reduce the cost of roaming, phone calls, and data usage.

While I am a firm believer in WiFi, below are some suggested ways to stay connected with your people back home. Whatever floats your boat!

If you need to call an international number, How To Call Abroad, helps you dial internationally with the correct country and area codes.

Recommended International Phone Plans:
- Google Fi
- Boingo
- AT&T
- T-Mobile
- NordVPN

If your phone is unlocked, you can also choose to purchase a local SIM card. Usually, the sales person at the mobile store will set everything up for you. This is usually the cheapest, yet most effective option.

Accommodations

Besides your typical hotel search engines like Kayak, Hotels, Priceline or Expedia. These home-sharing networks are usually budget-friendly, affordable and offer unique experiences in your local destination.

- *Airbnb:* I have a love/hate relationship with this site. I continue to go back because of its affordability. As long as you follow my tips, you should be fine.
- *Nomador:* Become a house sitter for homeowners all around the world. It may include some small duties like watching their pets, sometimes in exchange for free accommodation.
- *Trusted Housesitters:* Similar to Nomador, sign up to be a house sitter for individuals or families in destinations of your choice.

Blogs & Communities

WOMEN WHO TRAVEL

Let's be honest. Women are dominating the travel world and this domination is not slowing down anytime soon. Resources and stories for women by women are so important. Key information includes tips on safety, solo female travel, and travel advice. These are some of my favorite communities and blogs catered to women.

Recommended Resources:
- Traveling Black Women
- Pink Pangea
- On She Goes
- Wanderful

The Black Travel Movement

As women, the black travel movement is a force in the travel industry. Communities have given black people the resources, tools, and support needed to see the world as all other groups do.

Personally, as a Black Woman, I seek help and advice from online groups and online resources. Topics include traveling while black, safety tips, and recommendations for Black Women.

Weekend trip to San Sebastian

What to Expect

Warning: Don't do as I did and ignore the advice given to you by your pre-departure orientation leader.

During this period of time that you share with "experts" and/or students who have been in your shoes previously, PLEASE listen intently, take thorough notes, and believe everything they say. When abroad, you can adjust accordingly.

Prior to my departure to Spain, the study advisor sent out a notice to those participating in the summer program. During our planned meeting, the advisors went over information about the program, travel advice, first-time tips, and this new term, "culture shock".

I'm from Miami. What do I need to know about culture shock? - I thought. I'm around a lot of diversity already: Cubans, Haitians, Dominicans, etc. So, I brushed off that term as quickly as it had landed in my ears. But, I soon learned that arrogance has no place in studying abroad or traveling.

Culture Shock??!

The feeling of disorientation experienced by someone who is suddenly subjected to an unfamiliar culture, way of life, or set of attitudes.

Culture shock is real, but everyone experiences it differently and to varying degrees. Factors like socio-economic background, previous experiences, personality, fluency in the language, and social support systems can affect how long and deep culture shock can affect a person.

Stages of culture shock:

1. *Honeymoon stage:* Everything is new and exciting.
2. *Hostile and Irritable stage:* Some difficulties may occur and there may be feelings of impatience, anger, sadness, confusion, and frustration.
3. *Recovery stage:* You start to feel more relaxed. You're gaining some un-

derstanding of this new culture and finding balance in your new life abroad.

4. *Acceptance and integration:* You're adapting to the new culture and figuring out the good and bad things. You have a sense of belonging.

5. *Re-entry stage:* When you return home, things are not what they used to be.

Recognition of culture shock and at what stage allows an individual to address the challenges and adjust with minimal damage to mental health. Denial will only prolong the symptoms and make for a difficult time abroad.

Culture shock is normal! Once you realize this, you're able to work through it. Some suggestions include patience, looking for services or asking for help (i.e. friends, extracurricular activities, therapist), exercising, blogging, finding a community of new arrivals or a hobby, etc. These types of activities will help ease tension and boost mental health.

More than anything, a cultural adjustment improves soft skills, such as flexibility and adaptability, curiosity, communicativeness, and open-mindedness. Simply, just stick through the journey.

This is easier said than done. Sometimes, you're going to feel down, drained of energy, and regretful, but I say, take it one step at a time. That's what I did. I allowed myself to accept how I felt during the entire process. My peers and roommate could tell something was up, but I didn't know how to express myself.

"I didn't feel like they would understand."

After a few weeks in Spain, my roommate one night asked me why I never go out with her and the rest of the group. As we sat up in our beds, I looked at her and felt embarrassed.

What was I supposed to say???

"This has been a scary experience so far."
"I miss my family."
"I've never been this far away from home, I'm nervous about everything."
"This is hard..."

If the "me" now could whisper to the "me" then, I would've suggested that I said all of the above. There was nothing wrong with me admitting the truth. Denial will only prolong the shock and homesickness, but honesty will get you to a much better place sooner.

Some big culture shocks you may face:
- People staring at you
- Paying to use public restrooms
- No personal space
- Using non-western style toilets
- Strangers touching you or your hair (I know, a big no-no)
- Paying for items, such as condiments & plastic bags

But, that's not all...

Pros/Cons for Black Women

You'll face a different challenge living abroad:

Being Black AND a woman.

Don't be alarmed! Our hair has descended from a history of being misunderstood, outlawed, and now accepted (to an extent), so it's not surprising that we take our roots, regimen, and products very seriously. Yet, when traveling abroad, our hair can also lead to discriminatory practices.

TSA body scanners, for example, seem to discriminate against Black Women and our hair. Are they saying it's the wash-n-go, the coconut oil, or the bantu knots that are setting off the alarm on the scanner? Or, is there more to the story?

False alarms frequently occur when Black Women, who might wear braids or protective styles pass through their security scanner. Because of that, TSA Agents are more likely to conduct a more "thorough" search that includes a hair pat-down and inspection. This may seem harmless, but you know how we feel about people touching our hair. It's not only rude, but it can also be embarrassing.

Once, while traveling in Amsterdam, I was pulled to the side after moving through the body scanner and security line by a female agent and asked to check my hair. I had a twist-out that couldn't possibly hide any illegal or prohibited items. BUT, who am I to object when it's my hair versus my flight?

This is to scare you but to prepare you, in case you're stopped and asked to submit to a secondary screening. Just know, it's not you. It's most likely the scanners.

Tips to get through TSA:
- Wear your hair down (if done in braids, faux locs, or other protective styles)
- Don't get mad, you can ask the agent to change to a new pair of gloves before they touch your hair
- Hair pins will set the alarm off so avoid updo hairstyles that require them
- You may have to remove your scarf or turban (Sometimes they'll just squish it feeling what's underneath)

Hair Products

Just like your hair, your hair products may get flagged by the TSA agents. Be patient with them for they knoweth not what magic are in the bottles.

"Don't touch my hair
When it's the feelings I wear
Don't touch my soul
When it's the rhythm I know
Don't touch my crown
They say the vision I've found
Don't touch what's there
When it's the feelings I wear"
- Solange "Don't Touch My Hair"

It may be even more exhausting to navigate a new culture, communicate with the locals, take classes, and defend your identity. Not everyone will accept who you are and how you look. You might find that they may be:
- Curious about you because they've never seen a Black Woman before.
- Just ignorant.
- Sexually aroused
- Or, all of the above.

Whichever you encounter, set your boundaries, and own who you are.

In countless countries around the world, such as China and Buenos Aires, locals may approach you and ask to take your picture. This may seem flattering at first, but it can get annoying after awhile. Speak up and let them know whether you will take or continue to take photos. You do not have to submit to the pressure of the locals because you're in their country.

You may observe this more in rural and remote areas, than the major cities. Still, it's a lot to handle being bombarded with cameras and curious folks.

Beware of other situations where you may experience locals touching you with or without your permission. A student, who traveled to China for the first-time, revealed that the locals touched and rubbed her skin, sometimes more than once, because they thought it was dirt.

You may not find this amusing, but it's a reality you might face when traveling abroad. Start researching your host city, and see if you have to karate chop someone's hands (I'm half joking) to let them know NOT TO TOUCH YOU.

Other possible discriminatory and racist behaviors you might encounter:

- The assumption that you're a prostitute because you're a Black Woman in a space where there are few
- Being someone's fantasy and sexual fetish
- Consistent catcalling because of the above
- Getting called "Beyonce," "Chocolate Baby," "Brown Sugar," etc.
- Getting asked why your hair is so coily (especially if you're lighter-skinned)
- Told you're not American, simply because you're Black (Some countries believe that America is filled with only white people). Thanks, movie industry! *rolls eyes*

This isn't everything you might hear and it's also not restricted to international destinations. You may hear this stuff in your own neighborhood or on campus. *sips tea*

Anger and retaliation may seem like appropriate responses to these actions, but it can lead to unexpected consequences to your health, safety, and/or freedom. If you ever en-

*Independence Square
Accra, Ghana*

counter a dangerous, inappropriate, and/or unsafe situation, please report it to your program leader, advisor, or professor. There's no need for you to bear the weight of such atrocity. It's not your problem alone! Your advisor, program, or faculty leaders are obligated to take action.

Don't be deterred by what seems like inaction on their part. And, if you're ever made to feel like it was your fault or nothing can be done, send an email to your institution's study abroad advisor or even the Title IX coordinator ASAP!

Regardless, bad and good experiences can happen anywhere. To believe that Black people, in general, will only have negative encounters abroad is exaggerated and untrue. You, too, can have an amazing experience abroad and find acceptance and generosity in other parts of the world.

Born To Flex

"Even if it makes others uncomfortable, I will love who I am."
- Janelle Monáe

Embrace your identity, pop stereotypical bubbles, and push boundaries. Yours and others. Show up and show out about your Black culture. You also have a tremendous amount of experience and knowledge to add to the world, and you will not be shunned because of racist, malicious, or misogynistic people or stereotypes. Nor, should you allow your fears, doubts, and concerns to keep you from living your best life.

Most importantly, as a Black woman, you're not a trend. You're a trendsetter. You've been knocking down barriers and will continue to do so because your mind is your greatest resource.

Some of your greatest accomplishments will come from studying abroad, including:

1. *A unique skill set:* Stunt on 'em with your essential skills that you've improved and/or discovered while abroad. Such skills include interpersonal communication, problem-solving, empathy, flexibility, and adaptability that are useful and important traits when working with a diverse population. Working for companies like Google, you will feel valued as an employee for possessing these transferable skills that'll help you stand out as an emotionally intelligent person who is able to handle and adjust to any situation.

2. *Our Presence:* Let's be everywhere. Increase the presence of Black Women in the global marketplace. Everyday White people and legislators make decisions for us, without us. We have something to say too, but if we're not at the global table, how can we? Studying abroad, opens up opportunities by the mere presence and action of Black Women.

3. *It's value:* The value of studying abroad exceeds monetary gains. It's priceless.

4. *You're a Global Scholar:* Did you know that only 2% of U.S. students study abroad? That's right! You'll be part of a small group of students who'll ever get to use their studies to see the world. And, an even smaller percentage identifies as Black/African American. You will stand out.

5. *And, an Ambassador:* Your story means something. Your experience means everything. Share your experience, from deciding to and returning from studying abroad because it mat-

ters to the thousands of prospective black women looking for an opportunity to fulfill their dreams. Help them connect the dots. Pssst, and don't forget to mention the local beauty supply store in your host city. It's a lifesaver.

Resources for Your Identities

Black women come in all shapes, sizes, and skin tones alongside countless identities that will account for your experience abroad. I can't forget that you're also made up of some wonderful individual qualities that makes you, you.

Race & Ethnicity

WHAT TO CONSIDER: Consider the racial and ethnic groups that live in your host country/city, and if there is political or ethnic conflict presently. Also, think about how you will be perceived by the locals based on your race and ethnicity. With research, you should have some understanding about race relations in your destination.

To understand your race and ethnicity abroad, these are useful resources.

RECOMMENDATIONS:
- Diversity Abroad
- Black & Abroad

- Go Abroad - Diversity

First Generation

WHAT TO CONSIDER: Being classified as a first generation student is not a bad thing. In fact, being the first to go off to college in your family is empowering. Consider, however, what you don't know about studying abroad or what it means to travel. Basic isn't really so basic. Feel free to ask questions about the "how's," "why's," and "what's." It could be the difference between having an amazing or miserable time abroad.

To understand your first-generation status, these are useful resources.
- All Abroad
- I'm First!

LGBTQ+

WHAT TO CONSIDER: There are 73 countries with anti-homosexuality laws. Consider if your right to be LGBTQ+ outweighs living in a country with a religion and culture that undervalues your identity. Will you have to hide your identity to get access to living arrangements that are safe and open? Carefully research the laws, attitudes, and beliefs before making your decision.

RESOURCES
- U.S. Department of State - LGBTI Traveler Information
- International Gay & Lesbian Assc.
- GoAbroad - An LGBT Student Guide to Studying Abroad
- 76 Crimes
- Center for Black Equity

Gender

WHAT TO CONSIDER: Guess what? Only six countries in the world guarantee men and women equal rights. While the US is portrayed as the home of the land and free, we still have some growing and equaling to do. When evaluating cultural norms or expectations around the world regarding being a woman, find the similarities and differences and how that might affect your time abroad. Will this bias cause harm, danger, or worse?

RESOURCES
- Sexual Assault Support and Help for Americans Abroad

- CIEE - Women: What You Need To Know
- Information for Women Travelers - U.S. Department of State
- Women Abroad

Learning and/or Mobility Differences

WHAT TO CONSIDER: Living with a physical or mental mobility difference is nothing to be ashamed of. Just consider whether the study abroad can accommodate you based on the attention and resources you need. Consider what challenges can you prepare for and how will your host city view your difference.

RESOURCES
- Mobility International - Americans Going Abroad
- The University of Minnesota Learning Abroad Center - Students with Disabilities
- The Center for Disease Control - Traveler's Health
- Society for Accessible Travel & Hospitality

Faith & Religion

WHAT TO CONSIDER: Will your freedom of religion or non-religion be overlooked or demonized in your host city? Answering this question will show you how tolerant your study abroad destination is of other religions.

RESOURCES
- U.S. Department of State - International Religious Freedom Report
- Kahal: Your Jewish Home Abroad
- Diversity Abroad: Religion
- Interfaith Youth Core
- Religion and Spirituality Abroad

Non-Traditional

WHAT TO CONSIDER: If you're a non-traditional student, you're still more than welcome to study abroad. You might have more considerations if you have a family and work obligations. You may also need to consider if you would be a bit uneasy about studying abroad with traditional students. Think about your level of comfort and if there are programs specific to your needs.

Resources
- Adult Study Abroad
- Breaking Barriers
- Non-Traditional Scholarships

Strolling the streets of Santillana del Mar

Study Abroad Owes You Nothing:
Fun Ways to Get to Know Your Host City

*Previously published on www.Travepreneur.com
"The Black Woman's Guide to Solo Traveling."
Edited, modified and formatted for the purpose of this book.*

Imagine planning a trip to your favorite destination according to your own schedules, budget, and interests without having to string neither family nor friends along. No disappointment, no restrictions, no boundaries! Just you, ready to experience nature and the world at its finest. What could be more thrilling?

While traveling alone comes with sweet perks, the thought of it might scare you a little as a Black Woman. It can become rather overwhelming because there's so much to consider. The good news is, you don't need to stress because I've got you! No more missing out on travel opportunities simply because you're unsure of how to plan. Now is the best time to plan your first study abroad trip. Here are my personal tips and faves that'll guide you through everything you'd need to plan and experience your study abroad adventure:

Make Friends

Studying abroad doesn't mean you have to be by yourself all the time, it's going to get lonely. Good thing is, it doesn't have to be. There are apps that can help you meet new people and make friends while traveling. These apps (and Facebook groups) can also link you with a local that can serve as a travel guide:

- Meetup
- Show Around
- Flip The Trip
- Nearify

Security

For a Black Woman studying abroad, safety is one of the major issues you'll have to keep in check always. Trust your instincts. If your gut says something is off, it most probably is.

Stay polite and kind to the locals, but set

make your boundaries clear. Ensure that at least two people know your location at every point in time. The following apps can check in your location so your friends know where you are at every point:

- Swarm App
- Glimpse App

Whenever it's getting late or you feel like you have had a little too much alcohol, hail a cab to take you to your destination. Popular cab-hailing platforms available which can be downloaded on your mobile phone are:

- Uber
- Lyft
- OLA Cabs
- Juno

Always do the following when using an Uber or Lyft: (1) confirm the name of your driver; (2) verify the license plate. If it doesn't match, do not get into the vehicle; (3) share your ride with family and/or friends.

Things to Do

Apart from planned excursions with your study abroad program, get to know your host city through various activities.

Book a Tour

Studying Abroad in an unfamiliar territory can be confusing. You may need to book a tour to relieve you from the burden of having to discover everything by yourself. There's really no point in reinventing the wheel. Simply book a tour where you get to sit back, relax and enjoy the experience without any worries.

- Free Tours By Foot
- GPS My City
- Show Around
- Rent A Guide
- Viator
- Tours By Locals

*If you participate in a walking tour, be sure to download the Charity Miles app. It pays to move.

Document your Journey

One beautiful thing about traveling is that it gives you stories to tell and we know that stories shouldn't be hoarded, they should be shared. Aside from the commonly used social media platforms like Snapchat, Facebook, and

Instagram, there are many platforms that are specially designed to allow for travel journaling. You don't have to wait till you're back because you might miss out on some juicy details.

- Journi App
- BonJournal
- Day One App

Find the Good in Goodbye!

Whew! This is the part of the guide that'll help you explore what life is like after an amazing adventure to your study abroad destination. And, if you're here before you've even applied, then get back to work. The rest of us are waiting for you!

Truly, life after study abroad is just as rewarding as the actual experience. Yes, it's true you're no longer in your host city with your newfound friends (or lover, mmhmm!), but you've built a bond that a body of ocean can't even tear apart. I say that because with today's level of technology, you probably wouldn't be that affected by being in different countries or continents. Just think about the days when us older folk didn't have smartphones, and barely a video conferencing software to chat with others over the phone or computer. Thank God for modern tech.

I've Survived, Now what?!

Similar to Culture Shock, "Reverse Culture Shock" refers to the difficult and often unexpected transition process through which one progresses upon return to the home culture after an extensive sojourn in a different culture.

Students, upon their return home, expect a seamless transition. Assimilating back into your "old" environment may not be as easy. You've gained some perspective on yourself academically and culturally, and have spent a significant time abroad in your host city's culture and environment. Things have changed inside of you, which in turn changes your perspective on things that were once familiar. Your peers, your friends and family back home will see changes in you that you may not see.

If things feel off, or what was once comfortable and familiar seem foreign and strange, it's important to remember that this is normal. These are signs of what is known as reverse culture shock.

It's not a disease or a mental condition, but an emotional and maybe physical challenge of readjusting to home. Here are some stages of transition and re-entry challenges that will help you understand, interpret, and appreciate your time abroad and home.

Transition Stages

1. *Preparing to go home:* It was like yesterday when you arrived at your destination. You've appreciated the ups and downs and the experiences you've had. You realize that you will miss this place and the friends you've made while studying abroad. At the same time, you also miss your friends and family and are super excited to see them again and catch up with them about your journey. It's going to be bittersweet.

Challenges: Reverse "homesickness"

2. *The transition home:* The first few weeks that you're home, everyone is happy to see you and hear all of your stories. After a couple weeks to a month into your return, your friends and family are starting to change the subject whenever you bring up your study abroad experience.

> NOBODY:
> YOU: THAT TIME WHEN I LIVED IN (INSERT COUNTRY)...
> THEM: *ROLLS EYES*

You may feel frustrated and like a stranger in your own home. It may feel like it's difficult to communicate with others. You may code-switch between English and the foreign language you learned abroad. It's going to be tough, yet enlightening.

Challenges: No one wants to listen; relationships have changed; feelings of alienation

3. *The readjustment home:* You've been home for a while now and things are starting to feel normal again. But, you've adopted some new beliefs, attitudes, and habits as a result of your study abroad experience. Now you need to decide how to use them??

Challenges: How to apply new knowledge or skills; "lose" the experience.

Most importantly, life after studying abroad allows you space to reflect on things, such as your (1) personal growth, (2) career, and (3) purpose. You will survive.

> ALEXA, PLAY DESTINY'S CHILD "I'M A SURVIVOR"

*I'm a survivor, I'm gonna make it
I will survive, keep on survivin'*
-Destiny's Child

Take Time to Reflect

The challenges and transition stages are not permanent emotions or experiences that you will have upon your return home. Rather, these challenges give you space to reflect on major events that happen during the course of your study abroad program. This is why life after studying abroad is just as important as the experience itself. And, to get the most out of it, give yourself time to process and understand its impact.

For me, it took years to understand the value of my first and second study abroad experience. I, ultimately, set aside this amazing experience as if it was a book on a shelf. Part of the reason I didn't acknowledge my experience as valuable was the re-entry journey was never explained to me upon my return. Whether or not your study abroad advisor reaches out to you personally and as soon as you return, I'm here to tell you that you should evaluate your OWN international experience. Don't wait until someone asks you about your time abroad. Discover for yourself how might your personal, academic, and professional goals have changed.

HERE ARE SOME QUESTIONS TO USE IN YOUR REFLECTION:

Personal Growth

- What did you love most about being abroad? Why?
- What personal challenges did you face and how did you overcome them?
- What surprised you?

Career Outlook

- How did this study abroad experience change your career goals?
- How will you apply what you learned from your experience?
- What new skills did you pick up while abroad?

Purpose

- How did this study abroad experience

change your perspective, values, and/or view of the world and life?
- What will you do with this new perspective and experience?
- How do you plan to get involved in your community?

Re-entry checklist

This checklist will help you reflect, discover, and evaluate your study abroad program and experience, as well as give you insight into how you can market yourself for future opportunities, and to employers. Especially as a Traveling Black Woman.

- Understand the term and process of "re-entry"
- Read the stages of transition and re-entry challenges
- REFLECT [this will take the longest]
- Find a Black women's travel group!! Share with others seeking advice on where to travel and how to make it a reality. Become an expert!
- Visit the Career Office at your university. Seek guidance on how to link your study abroad experience to spe-

- cific skills and careers.
- Update your resume and cover letter to include your global experience.
- Find possible internships or opportunities as a study abroad alumna.
- Engage with potential study abroad students. Whether as a peer advisor or speaker/presenter. (See your Study Abroad Office for more details)
- Stay connected to your host country/culture

Keep Evolving

Want to practice sharing what you've learned or experienced with other Black women, future employers, or graduate schools? To be able to articulate what studying abroad means, not just personally, but also professionally?

Then use this space to pull out the important moments and lessons from abroad!

Think critically about how each component ties to your goals and your skills. This will become your story. Your trademark into how you've studied abroad regardless of the obstacles, challenges, culture shock, homesickness, whatever.

In each section, write about a lesson you

learned during your experience, and include a skill or attribute that you can tie to this specific experience.

What common themes, lessons, or trends do you see in your story?

·Courses:

-

-

-

-

·Housing·

·Social Life·

·Identity·

· *Other.·*

Additional Resources

1. Term to Know
- Culture Shock: The anxiety and feelings (of surprise, disorientation, confusion, etc.) one feels when coming into contact with an entirely different social environment, such as a different country. It often relates to the temporary inability to assimilate to the new culture, causing difficulty in knowing what is appropriate and what is not.

2. Scholarships & Fellowships
- Benjamin A. Gilman International Scholarship
- Fulbright
- Fund for Education Abroad
- Diversity Abroad
- BeGirl World
- Boren Fellowships

3. Budget Tips Checklist
- Find flights with Skyscanner
- Plan to travel during the week, instead of the weekend

- Book with Budget Airlines
- Open a bank account with no debit or credit card transaction fees.

4. More Reading

- https://www.diversityabroad.com/guides/study-abroad-guide/what-is-study-abroad-
- https://www.isepstudyabroad.org/articles/225
- Need ideas on how to raise money or save for you study abroad program? https://theabroadguide.com/ways-to-save-money-study-abroad/
- https://www.nerdwallet.com/blog/banking/debit-card-foreign-transaction-international-atm-fees/
- Healthyway - Culture Shock: https://www.healthyway.com/content/pushing-through-the-crisis-tips-for-dealing-with-culture-shock/

5. For Parents

- Now, parents are rightfully concerned about a lot of things like your health, safety, and future. But, when you go off to college, additional factors like cost and program security become a major concern too.

Manifest & Glow.
You got this!

Sincerely,

Adriana

About the Author

Adriana, a blogger and educator, was embarrassed when she got lost in Madrid during the first two days of her study abroad program. She immediately wanted to book a flight home, but couldn't as she was a first-generation student with no extra money. Yet, that moment defined her entire travel journey. She discovered a new perspective to life: humility and global citizenry. Blown away by the rewarding experience, she devoted her personal and professional development to connecting purposefully to each and every country and city. She later volunteered in Quito, which inspired the launch of *Travepreneur*. Catering to new, minority travelers, she empowers us all to be Social Do-Gooders Traveling the World.

@travepreneur
Travepreneur.com

Additional publications:

Catalyst - Volunteering:
- http://catalyst.com/i-didnt-want-to-volunteer-abroad-but-im-glad-i-did/2017/12/5/i-didnt-want-to-volunteer-abroad-but-im-glad-i-did?rq=volunteering

Givingway - Volunteering:
- https://www.givingway.com/blog/my-experience-as-a-black-woman-volunteering-abroad/

P.S. Don't try to impress someone who never studied abroad.
PERIODT

www.travelingblackwomen.com

www.ingramcontent.com/pod-product-compliance
Lightning Source LLC
LaVergne TN
LVHW070048070526
838201LV00036B/354